25/9/2000

IMAGES
*of England*

# MINING IN CORNWALL
# VOLUME THREE:
# PENWITH AND SOUTH KERRIER

For Mark, Katie, Jack and Sophie
who inherit the proud tradition of
their Cornish ancestry.

IMAGES
*of England*

# MINING IN CORNWALL
# VOLUME THREE:
# PENWITH AND SOUTH KERRIER

*Compiled by*
L.J. Bullen

TEMPUS

Tempus Publishing Limited
The Mill, Brimscombe Port,
Stroud, Gloucestershire, GL5 2QG

ISBN 0 7524 1759 2

Typesetting and origination by
Tempus Publishing Limited
Printed in Great Britain by
Midway Clark Printing, Wiltshire

Botallack Mine, Allen's Shaft. The electric pump station at 1,230ft from the surface in a photograph by A.J. Fellows taken on 26 September 1913.

# Contents

# Acknowledgements

The following persons have helped me in a variety of ways in the preparation of this photographic review. I would like to express my thanks for their kind assistance:

Tony S. Bennett; John Brooks, National Trust; Andrew Davey, National Trust; Tom Murray; Bill North; Andrew Payne; John Peck; Paul Richards; Michael Shipp; Anne Smith; Robert Smith; Milton Thomas; John Treloar; Geoff Treseder.

I also wish to thank my publishers for their encouragement and support.

The Kenidjack Valley in 1922. Tin streamers and their make-do-and-mend equipment during a period of deep recession in the industry. Power is provided for a buddle using a wheel from a pony trap with corned beef tins to form a water wheel. The boys were paid 7s 6d (37.5 p) per week. From left to right: Bill Semmens, William Nicholls, Jim Nicholls, John Williams, B.J. Keast.

# Introduction

This book covers most of the Penwith and South Kerrier areas of Cornwall but some mines have not been included due to space restriction. These will be dealt with in a later volume.

The Penwith peninsula constitutes one of the major mining areas of Cornwall from which a prodigious quantity of tin has been won. It is the second largest producer of this metal in the Duchy after the Camborne/Redruth/St Day district. The output of copper has also been significant. Among other minerals recorded are arsenic (as a by-product of tin), china clay and a small tonnage of iron ore. Any further mineral returns have been relatively small.

A considerable number of hitherto unpublished photographs appear in this book. It is hoped that the contents will encourage the reader to seek further information about the mines portrayed. They will find their research very rewarding.

L.J. Bullen, Camborne, Cornwall – April 2000

Geevor Tin Mines Ltd, Victory Shaft and the mill in a picture showing the large stockpiles of graded gravel, *c*.1980. This was a saleable by-product of the milling operations which was purchased by local authorities, builders, etc.

# One
# St Just to Penzance

Bellan Mine, Cot Valley, St Just, *c*.1943. The erection of a small tin treatment plant during the Second World War.

Bellan Mine, Cot Valley, St Just. A further view of the plant, *c.*1943.

Wheal Owles, St Just. A view of the collar of the Cargodna Shaft after the accident on 10 January 1893. Twenty miners lost their lives in the flooding and their bodies were never recovered. A policeman can be seen on the left of the photograph. This tragedy was caused by an error in surveying. The flooded workings of the adjacent Wheal Drea were penetrated because the mine surveyor had failed, over many years, to allow for the variation in magnetic North.

Wheal Hermon, St Just. A view of the Main Shaft in the early twentieth century. This is a most interesting little mine worked anciently and re-opened around 1910 by a mining engineer who had returned to England from India. His tragic death caused by falling down this shaft brought operations to a halt. In a different metals market to that pertaining at present, this mine is considered to be a good prospect.

St Just United Mine, Bailey's Shaft. A photograph taken looking across Priests cove showing the mine before the steam stamps had been erected. The configuration of the winding engine and pumping engine houses had the very unusual arrangement of the headgear with the long boom stays straddling the pumping engine house. Photograph by Gibson, c.1881

St Just United Mine. A slightly later picture of the mine (late nineteenth century), showing, from left to right: Burning house stack, stamps engine, Bailey's Shaft headgear and 36-in cylinder pumping engine and the winding engine. The Count House is to the right of the road. Cape Cornwall and the buildings of its then abandoned mine form the background.

St Just United Mine. This picture from the early 1880's shows the newly-erected stamps engine.

St Just United Mine, Bailey's Shaft, *c.*1881. A close-up view of the house containing the 36-in cylinder pumping engine with its boiler house and separate stack. The very high headgear is surmounted by a tripod which was used to change the sheave wheels or replace bearings.

St Just Foundry at Tregaseal during the 1890's. Holman's Foundry had a high reputation for excellent workmanship. They were cousins of the famous Holman Bros Ltd of Camborne. The compressed air hoist installed underground on New Submarine Shaft at the Levant Mine was designed by G. Eustice and built by this foundry.

Wheal Edward, St Just. The stamps and, in the background, the pumping engine house in an image from the late nineteenth century.

Cape Cornwall Mine, *c*.1870. A view taken shortly after the mine closed. The pumping engine house is on the left with the winding engine house in the centre. To the right is the Count House. The stack on top of the Cape, which is still a prominent landmark, created too much draught for the winding engine boiler. A shorter stack was then built much lower down the slope and can be seen in this print.

Cape Cornwall Mine, 1966. A diamond drilling programme was undertaken by St Just Mining Services (a consortium of Union Corporation and Geevor Tin Mines Ltd) to examine the prospects of the mine. This photograph shows the drilling rig between the former Count House and the building constructed on the site of the former boiler house for the winding engine. The Brisons can be seen in the background-scene of many a shipwreck in the olden days.

Cape Cornwall Mine, a closer view of the diamond drill rig taken in the summer of 1966.

Boswedden Mine. A view looking towards Cape Cornwall at the seaward end of the Nancherrow Valley. A great deal of historic information was destroyed when a cloudburst flooded this valley many years ago. Photograph by Gibson, late nineteenth century.

Boswedden Mine. Another late-nineteenth-century view looking towards Cape Cornwall in this highly industrialized valley. The mine had an incline shaft which ran under the sea.

Botallack Mine, mid-nineteenth century. An engraving showing the Crowns section when at work. The beam winding engine at the top of the cliff operated a vertical axis drum through bevel gears. This was a very early type of beam winder.

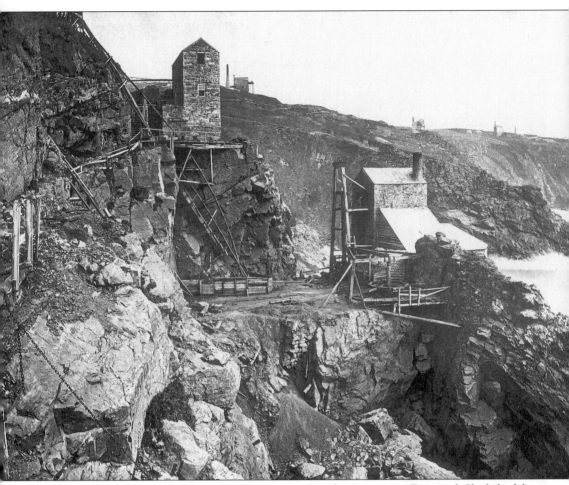

Botallack Mine, 1870's. The Crowns section after the Boscawen Diagonal Shaft had been abandoned. The pumping engine is still at work providing dressing water for the stamps. The pump columns can be seen rising up the cliff face on the left. It will be noted that this pipeline is going down a shaft some distance to the left of the engine shaft. Apparently these two shafts met like a letter Y in depth. The winding engine house is beginning to look derelict and its boiler house is roofless. The skip road and supporting trestle which would have dominated the scene have been dismantled. In the background, immediately to the right of the winding engine house, the stamps engine house of Botallack and stack can be seen. This engine has two beams: the left-hand beam drove the stamps axle and the right-hand pumped from Narrow Shaft. On the skyline over the stack of the pumping engine can be seen the pumping engine of Wheal Edward. To its right is the engine house of Wheal Edward stamps.(See earlier photograph on page 22.)

Botallack Mine, Wheal Cock section, Skip Shaft, 1880's. Note the number of guy ropes and chains bracing this tall headgear. This structure was in a very exposed position on Cornwall's Atlantic Coast, which is dramatically illustrated by the photograph on page 21.

Botallack Mine, Boscawen Diagonal Shaft, 24 July 1865. The occasion was the visit of the Prince and Princess of Wales (later King Edward VII and Queen Alexandra) when they travelled underground through this shaft. The decorative greenery was in honour of the royal couple.

Botallack Mine, 1 October 1907 during the re-working that took place between 1907 and 1914. The mine had a Fowler Traction Engine which is seen here outside Penzance Railway Station. On the trailers are parts of the new Holman-built steam winding engine for the Allen's Shaft which was being sunk at that time. Photograph by A.J. Fellows.

Botallack Mine, Wheal Cock section, Skip Shaft, 1880's. This dramatic photograph clearly illustrates the lofty perch of the headgear. On the right the engine house on Engine Shaft is visible. Photograph by Gibson.

Botallack Mine, Boscawen Diagonal Shaft. An artist's impression of the large number of people who thronged the cliffs to see the Prince and Princess of Wales during their visit on 24 July 1865.

Botallack Mine, Boscawen Diagonal Shaft, 1865. This shows the trestle which led down to the shaft portal and the house which contained the beam winding engine. In the background on the left hand side is the top of the headgear on Wheal Hazard Shaft.

Botallack Mine, c.1908. On the left of the picture may be seen the Power Station which housed the gas engines and generators to provide electrical power for the mine. The stack and boiler of the temporary winder on Allen's Shaft are on the centre skyline. The framing for the Californian stamps is being erected and many of the fabrications for the new mill are in the foreground. This view was taken quite early in the re-working of the mine between 1907 and 1914. It should be noted that the main winding engine on the new Allen's Shaft was steam-powered.

Botallack Mine, c.1908. The Count House and weighbridge house are on the right. In the background are the new workshops and traction engine house. The Fowler Traction Engine can be seen by these buildings.

Botallack Mine, Wheal Cock Engine Shaft. The new headgear and electric sinking pump during the early part of the 1907-1914 re-working.

Botallack Mine, 9 September 1908. Allen's Shaft winding engine house and stack being erected during the 1907-1914 re-working. Photograph by A.J. Fellows.

Botallack Mine. The derelict stamps engine house. The stamps were on the other side of the house and the bob wall facing the camera carried a beam which pumped water for dressing purposes from Narrow Shaft. The figures are Penzance School of Mines students carrying out a survey. The photograph was taken around 1904 when the mine was still disused.

Botallack Mine, Wheal Cock Engine Shaft, *c.*1908. The headgear for the electric sinking pump. Note the terminal pole of the electric overhead supply line built from the new Generating Station.

Botallack Mine, *c.*1912. From left to right: roof of Mill building, tramway gantry to ore bin, headgear on Allen's Shaft and buildings for the horizontal steam winder and boilers. There was one Lancashire boiler with space for a second. A large vertical boiler was used for steaming the winder when the Lancashire boiler was being cleansed.

Botallack Mine, Wheal Cock Section, c.1908. A ladderway constructed in the zawn below Wheal Cock Engine Shaft for access to the adit.

Botallack Mine, Allen's Shaft, the sinking headgear, c.1908. In the background is the scaffolding around the stack being built for the permanent steam winder.

Botallack Mine, Wheal Cock Engine Shaft, *c.*1908. The electric pump is ready to be lowered.

Botallack Mine, Allen's Shaft, 22 August 1912. The permanent winder and headgear when the mine was in production. Photograph by A.J. Fellows.

Botallack Mine, Allen's Shaft, August 1908. The collar of the shaft during sinking operations. The figure on the left is the late A.J. Fellows, the photographer.

Botallack Mine, Allen's Shaft, c.1907. A view of the collar of the new shaft which eventually reached a depth of 1,477ft. It was one of the largest shafts ever sunk in the county, being 19ft and 6in by 6ft within timbers and having five compartments.

Botallack Mine, *c.*1908. Delivery of parts of the suction gas engines to the Generator House on the right. The Californian Mill building is in the background.

Botallack Mine, *c.*1908. The new Mill building under construction. Photograph by J.C. Burrow.

Botallack Mine, *c*.1900. After the mine closed in 1895, the Penzance School of Mines took a lease on the Count House and some other buildings as a base for their survey department. These students are seen here while undergoing instruction.

Botallack Mine, Wheal Cock section, early 1890's. The engine shaft is visible on the left, with the skip shaft on the right. This print illustrates once again the windswept position of the headgear on skip shaft.

Botallack Mine, Nineveh Shaft, *c.*1909. Refurbishing of the shaft for pumping. The 'four-poster' transformer pole on the left is the terminal pole for the line which brought power from the Generating Station. Over the shaft is a wooden headgear. In the foreground is a small steam winch and vertical boiler used for lowering the electric pump. The horse on the right seems content to rest from his labours!

Botallack Mine, Boscawen Diagonal Shaft, *c.*1870. This picture shows the inclined trestle from the winding engine to the shaft portal which carried the tramway into the mine. Note the 'flat sea' caused by the wet plate negative process at the time.

Botallack Mine, Allen's Shaft, *c.*1909. The stack for the winding engine boiler is being built. A pond for feed water and the leat and launders which supply it are complete. The winding engine house is under construction and in the background can be seen the top of the temporary sinking headgear on the shaft and the roof of the Generating Station.

Botallack Mine, Allen's Shaft, *c.*1908. The concrete shaft collar is in the middle of the picture. To the left is the Generating Station which appears to be very near completion. In the foreground are two wooden fabrications of a headgear awaiting erection.

Botallack Mine, *c*.1907. The commencement of the operations in the last re-working of the mine early in the twentieth century. The Electricity Generating Station is being built on the right.

Botallack Mine, *c*.1909. An internal view of the Generating Station. Originally it was thought that three gas engines of 150hp each would be sufficient. However, it was eventually decided to substitute the third engine with one of 315hp.

Botallack Mine, *c.*1908. Another view taken early in the 1907-1914 re-working showing a temporary tram road in use. On the left the framing for the Californian stamps is being erected and the Generating Station is in an advanced state of construction in the background.

Botallack Mine, early twentieth century. The magazine where explosives were stored was, for obvious reasons, sited well away from other buildings. This is the prototypical circular Cornish magazine. Note the lightning conductor.

Botallack Mine, *c*.1908. The heavy framing for the Californian stamps can be seen in the foreground while under construction. On the left the Generating Station is nearing completion. The gas engines and dynamos will be housed in the left hand building. The gas producers will be erected in the lean to building.

Botallack Mine, *c*.1908. The vertical boiler and stack for the Allen's Shaft temporary sinking winder is in the centre. On the right, the Generating Station is already roofed.

Botallack Mine, *c.*1908. The Count House and associated buildings are seen here when being refurbished in the last re-working. Two of the traction engine waggons can also be seen in this view.

Levant Mine, early 1920's. On the skyline to the left is the stack of the Power Station and compressors smoking heavily. In the centre are the remains of the walls of the old Cornish stamps with its stack still standing. The big dump running out to the right was used to tram the ore to the new stamps. The arsenic chimney is smoking left of centre. On the extreme right are the buildings of the first part of the new mill which consisted of five head of Californian stamps and two head of Nissen stamps. The buildings in the foreground are part of Geevor Mine.

Levant Mine, c.1923. Taken from lower down the cliffs looking upwards at the complex around Skip and Engine Shafts.

Levant Mine, mid-nineteenth century. A very old print showing, on the left, an engine house which was thought wound from a shaft on the other side of the zawn. The arsenic stack is in the background. The middle ground is occupied by a small engine house believed to have driven the copper crusher. On the right are the winding and pumping engine houses on Skip Shaft and Engine Shaft.

Levant Mine, mid-1920's. A general view of Skip and Engine Shafts. It will be noticed that the boiler house of the winding engine is partly demolished. At this time, in the final years of the life of the mine, the management could not afford to replace the boiler and the steam pipe from the pumping engine boilers was used to steam the winder on a permanent basis.

Levant Mine . The Cornish stamps when still at work. Photograph by H.G. Ordish, 1920.

Levant Mine. The trestle from Skip Shaft to the ore bin with an unusual load! This picture was taken a short while after the mine had ceased working in the early 1930's.

Levant Mine, Skip Shaft, 1927. An internal view of the totally enclosed beam winder which hauled on the shaft. The sweep rod connecting the nose of the beam to the crank on the shaft of the winding drums can be seen on the left. On the wall is the circular depth indicator for the skips. The driver can just be discerned on the right. Photograph by H.G. Ordish.

Levant Mine. The new mill under construction in the 1920's. The long dump leading to the new mill and carrying a tramway is visible in the background. To the right of the new buildings the four Brunton calciners are visible and in the background the arsenic stack can also be seen.

The Levant Mine in the 1960's. At that time, a Consortium, which included Geevor Tin Mines Ltd, undertook a re-evaluation of Levant. It was found that the Atlantic Ocean had broken into the mine during the period since it closed in 1930. The breach had occurred at the 40-backs level. Reed-Malik were awarded the contract for the major task of sealing out the sea from the mine. Skip Shaft was reconditioned and a headgear and electric winder installed. The silo for cement for the prodigious amount of concrete grout required can be seen on the right. In the background is Pendeen lighthouse.

Levant Mine, 1960's. An early view of the work on Skip Shaft in connection with the sealing of the 40-backs level. This shows the headgear and electric winder house with the old pumping and winding engine houses in the background. Later on the headgear was rotated through 180° and a larger winder installed when the shaft was refurbished in depth. The great dry-stone wall is original and a remarkable piece of workmanship.

Levant Mine, 1960's. A little later view of the Skip Shaft when the larger winder had been installed. This can be seen to the right of the roofless old pumping-engine house. All the remaining new buildings were erected at this time.

Levant Mine, 1960's. A view of the complex of buildings, old and new, around Skip and Engine Shafts. This photograph was taken during operations in Skip Shaft when the sea was sealed from the 40-backs level. At the same time, much dangerous sea bed work was also undertaken by divers operating from a vessel off the coast.

Levant Mine. A view of the buildings around Skip and Engine Shafts in 1922. The left-hand building contained the beam winding engine which still exists and is preserved by the National Trust in working condition. The wooden headgear on the Skip Shaft is between the winding and pumping engine houses. By this time the winder was taking steam from the pumping engine boilers. The photographer was the late J.H. Trounson who, at the age of seventeen, had cycled from Redruth – a round trip of nearly fifty miles! His bicycle can be seen leaning against the right-hand wall.

Levant Mine. A much older view (c.1900) of Skip and Engine Shafts. A steam pipe is linking the pumping engine boiler house with the winding engine boiler house suitably clad in asbestos. This was initially an innovation to keep the winder working when its solitary boiler was being cleansed or repaired. At a later date, when the winder boiler was condemned, this arrangement became permanent as funds were not available for a replacement boiler.

Levant Mine, the Cornish stamps, *c*.1890. A rare print of the stamps showing how the bob (or beam) had been strengthened at some time.

Levant Mine,1931. A general view of Engine Shaft and Skip Shaft taken from the seaward side just after operations ceased.

Levant Mine, early 1930's. Engine Shaft. This picture, showing the beam of the 45-in pumping engine after being thrown down from the bob wall, was taken at the time when the machinery was being scrapped.

Levant Mine, early 1930's. The scrapping of the pumping engine. On the left is the late Captain W.H. Ellis former underground Agent at the mine.

Levant Mine, *c.*1890. A large group of men and boys outside the Count House on pay day.

Levant Mine, *c.*1920. A view of the dressing floors. In the foreground are round frames and behind on the right are the calciners and the arsenic stack. On the skyline is the Cornish stamps engine house and stack.

Levant Mine, 1890's. Under the sea. The miners are sinking a winze (or sub-shaft).

LEVANT MINE, PENDEEN, NR. PENZANCE. 33.

Levant Mine. Another view of the dressing floors from the early 1920's. On the left the new mill is being built and, to its right, is the tall arsenic stack. A little further right are the Brunton calciners. The first plant to be installed in the new mill were, as previously stated, five head of Californian stamps and two of Nissen stamps. These had been purchased from the Tincroft Mine at Pool, near Redruth.

Levant Mine, Engine Shaft, *c.*1927. The pumping engine is working. Note the surface balance box alongside the boiler house. Photograph by H.G. Ordish.

Levant Mine in the early twentieth century. An inside view of the house of the 45-in pumping engine showing the gearwork. Photograph by W. Michell.

Levant Mine, c.1900. An underground-view of the Man engine Shaft. The rod of the engine can be seen on the right with the hand grip. The step on which the miner stood is just below the feet of the central figure. The 'knocker line' handle is in the centre of the photograph. This wire line ran through the depth of the shaft and was used to signal the driver of the engine at surface. The man engine conveyed men from surface to the 266 fathom level. It consisted of a continuous rod with steps or platforms at 12-ft intervals, i.e. the length the rod moved per stroke. When it was in use, the miners stepped on to the rod from fixed platforms in the shaft also at 12-ft spacing. In this way they could travel up and down the shaft as they wished. This was the intermediate means of gaining access to the underground workings. Prior to this, men and boys had to climb the ladders and later they were conveyed in cages which ran on guides in the shaft.

Levant Mine, Old Submarine Shaft at the 278 fathom level. This was a sub-shaft sunk during the nineteenth century to exploit the tin lodes even deeper. This photograph was taken after the mine had been de-watered and when the re-opening of Levant was a distinct possibility. Photograph by Tom Murray, October 1982.

51

The Balleswidden China Clay Works in the early 1920's. The sky tip for waste operated by a self-dumping skip on the inclined tramway.

Geevor Mine, Wheal Carne Shaft in the early 1920's.

Geevor Mine, a general view of the Wethered Shaft taken in the early 1920's.

Geevor Mine, Victory Shaft. Taken shortly after the shaft came into production, this picture from the early 1920's shows the wooden headgear and the buildings containing the horizontal steam winder and compressors. The stack served the boilers which steamed the winding engine. The aerial ropeway between Wethered Shaft and the mill can be seen.

Geevor Mine, Pig Shaft, c.1900. This was an old shaft north-north west of Wethered Shaft and is considered to be the beginning of Geevor Tin Mines Ltd. This is an excellent illustration of a horse whim and associated poppet heads (headgear).

Geevor Mine, a general view of Victory Shaft from the early 1920's.

Geevor Mine. Taken just after the end of the First World War, this picture shows the terminal station of the aerial ropeway from Wethered Shaft and some of the mill buildings. In the foreground is a pair of winding drums. These were part of the steam winding engine which was eventually erected on the Victory Shaft shortly to be commenced just to the right of this photograph. The engine was second-hand when purchased by the Wheal Vor Company in the abortive re-opening of that mine. It was bought by Geevor for their planned new shaft.

Geevor Mine, Victory Shaft. The horizontal steam winder at work in the late 1940's. During the Second World War, the engine was partially re-built with two new winding drum sides manufactured by Bartle's of Carn Brea, Redruth, and post brakes which greatly improved the braking. When this engine ceased work in 1956, at the time of the commissioning of the new electric winder it had served the mine for about thirty-six years.

Geevor Mine, Victory Shaft. The new electric winder house under construction in the mid-1950's. In the background can be seen the wooden headgear which was replaced at this time with a much higher steel structure.

Geevor Mine, Victory Shaft, mid-1950's. The new steel headgear is nearly completed and is towering above the original wooden structure. The new electric winder house appears to be complete.

Geevor Mine, Victory Shaft, mid-1950's. The wooden headgear is still in use together with the steam winder. The frame of the new electric winder house is in the background. It can be noticed that the wooded headgear legs have been reinforced hence the necessity for a replacement headgear.

Another view of Geevor Mine, Victory Shaft from the same period. Taken from below the complex this picture shows the new steel headgear and electric winder in service.

Victory Shaft at Geevor Mine, sub incline, *c.*1976. Sinking winder used by Thyssen's the contractors and later replaced by a permanent winder. The track on the incline was 40lb/yd and the gauge was 36in.

Geevor Mine, Victory Shaft and the mill, mid 1930's. This photograph was taken from the site of the former Levant Mine Mill.

Geevor Mine, 9 September 1908, the first mill built by the mine. The old North Levant Mine stamps engine house is visible. This had been cut down but the chimney was left standing. The pneumatic stamp at Geevor was driven by a steam engine and boiler utilizing this old stack. This unique print shows the very early operations by Geevor in the twentieth century. Photograph by A.J. Fellows.

Geevor Mine, Victory Shaft, c.1930. An early view of the headgear, winder and compressor houses. The enclosed gantry carries the tramway to the mill.

Geevor Mine, Victory Shaft, 1964. The electric winder in the background replaced the steam winder in 1956. A new house was erected over the steam winder as it was utilized until the mine closed for changing ropes on the new hoist when required. Compressed air was used for this operation.

Geevor Mine, Wethered Shaft. This scene from the 1950's shows the clearing of North Levant Mine burrows in preparation for the building of Geevor 33,000 volt to 11,000 volt electricity substation by the South Western Electricity Board. The Wethered Shaft winding engine house and headgear are in the background. The figure on the left in overalls and boots is the late G. Corkell, foreman of the site operations.

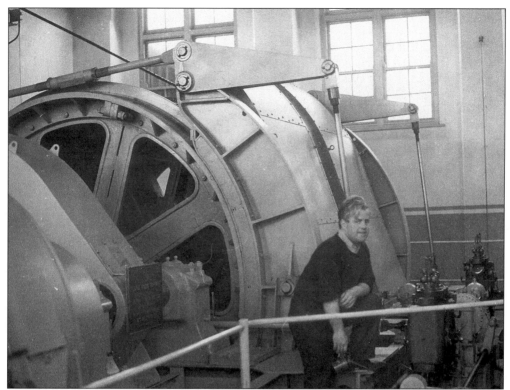

Geevor Mine, Victory Shaft, July 1964. The electric hoist, built by the British Thomson Houston Co., was installed in 1956 to replace the steam winder.

Boscaswell Downs Mine, North Boscaswell Section, Trease Shaft. In or about 1907 an attempt was made to re-open this part of the mine. The scene shows the headgear and the buildings of the small mill. The East Pool & Agar mine near Redruth had a lease on Boscaswell Downs in the 1930's. The late J.H. Trounson visited the property and went underground taking samples. He probably took this photograph in 1932.

Boscaswell Downs Mine, North Boscaswell Section, Trease Shaft. A further view thought to have been taken in 1914.

Boscaswell Downs Mine, North Boscaswell Section, c.1907. A small plant on Trease Shaft prior to the erection of the headgear and the other buildings shown in the previous picture.

Boscaswell Downs Mine, Treweeks Shaft, 1964. The Geevor mine unwatered Boscaswell Downs Mine and in the 1960's rehabilitated Treweeks shaft as access for men and materials only. This photograph shows work in progress when sinking a short length of inclined shaft to connect with Treweeks Shaft. The original shaft was a compound, i.e. vertical from surface and then on the underlie (inclined). It was decided for ease of shaft arrangements to make the shaft underlie from surface. The old shaft collar is under the tripod in the foreground. The new collar is being formed in the background.

Boscaswell Downs Mine, Treweeks Shaft, 1964. The new shaft collar is here clearly visible.

Boscaswell Downs Mine, Treweeks Shaft, 1964. A general view of the site showing the electric winder and the new house being built. Both the old and new shaft collars are visible on the right.

A further view of Boscaswell Downs Mine, Treweeks Shaft, c.1965, showing the now completed and fully-operational plant with ancillary buildings.

The East Botallack Mine in the late nineteenth century. A small mine the site of which is still visible beside the main road from Penzance to St Just. The stack and boiler house are on the left. A horizontal steam winding/pumping engine is in the wooden building behind the headgear. On the other side of the road, on the extreme left, is the blacksmiths shop and, to the right, the miners' dry (change house) and carpenters shop.

Carnelloe Mine, No.1 Shaft, 1937. Captain W. Ellis, formerly of Levant Mine, is standing by the shaft collar. Note the wooden guides for the skip. The ore was drawn up the shaft and over the cliff face by a hoist driven by a waterwheel.

Carnelloe Mine, No.1 Shaft, 1937. Tommy Trembath is clearing the debris covering the planks at the shaft collar.

Carnelloe Mine, 1936. Sampling a portion of the 'big cut'. A leat runs from the south-west boundary to a point above this cut where a small reservoir exists for the supply of water for sluicing.

Morvah Consols Mine, the remains of the beam rotary engine house in a 1934-photograph by H.G. Ordish.

*Following pages:* Gurnards Head Mine. This photograph was taken by Gibson in the mid-nineteenth century and shows the house on Engine Shaft and, on the left, the Count House. The figure on the left is one of the famous Gibson family of well-known Cornish photographers. The little vehicle carries a portable kit for the development and sensitising of their wet plate negatives.

Ding Dong Mine. The Greenburrow Shaft in a picture by A.J. Fellows taken on 23 September 1907. The pumping engine house and stack were still in quite good condition at the time this photograph was taken. The timbers of the unusual hip roof are in place although most of the slates have blown off.

Rosevale Mine. A photograph taken by R.A. Smith in 1983 showing the shaft on the adit when being refurbished.

Rosevale Mine in the late 1980's. This photograph was taken by T.S. Bennett and it shows No.2 level with stull timbers and 24-in gauge tramway.

Rosevale Mine, No.1 Level. Note the ladderway protruding from the winze down to No.2 level. Tony Bennett is using a pneumatic drill. The photograph was taken in the late 1980's by John Peck.

Another picture by T.S. Bennett from the late 1980's showing Rosevale Mine, No.2 level portal. Battery electric locomotive and train are emerging from the mine.

Rosevale Mine, 1994. Unloading a waggon which had been trammed out of No.2 Level. A minor collapse of kaolinized ground was being cleared. The figure on the right is Mike Shipp who took up the lease and commenced refurbishing the mine in 1974 as a hobby. He has been involved ever since and at any one time there has never been more than two or three persons doing the practical and heavy work. For many years Mrs Joan Sheldrake was one of the team. Photograph by John Peck.

The Wherry Mine, Penzance. An old print from the mid-nineteenth century depicting the mine in the second and last re-working which ceased in 1840. The mine was kept dry by a beam rotary engine driving flat rods along the pier to the shaft.

The Wherry Mine, 1967. A diamond drilling programme was carried out on the stanniferous elvan at the Wherry Rocks off the Penzance sea front. This was to assess the possibilities of re-working the mineral deposit. In this view is the long scaffolding pier built to obtain access from the shore.

The Wherry Mine. A further view from 1967 showing the pier and drill rig.

# Two
# The St Ives Area

St Ives Consolidated Mines Ltd. Giew electric Power Station was built when the Central Power Station closed in 1916, probably the same year this photograph was taken. It worked for only a short time after which a supply was taken from the Cornwall Electric Power Co. Generating Station at Hayle. The original winding and pumping engine houses are prominent.

BACK OF MILL, ROBINSON'S HEAD GEAR, CRUSHER, HOIST HOUSE AND GANTRY. GIEW
ST. IVES CONSOLIDATED LTD.

St Ives Consolidated Mines Ltd. Giew section, *c.*1912. The scene is adequately described in the print.

*Following page:* St Ives Consolidated Mines Ltd. Giew section. Frank's Shaft early in the twentieth-century re-working (*c.*1909). The pitwork of the old pumping engine was still in the shaft below adit level. It was decided to un-water the mine by erecting a wooden beam on the bob wall of the engine house which was to be powered with an electric motor driving a geared crank placed inside the house. The new pitwork placed in the upper part of the shaft was connected to the existing pitwork and the mine was successfully pumped out by this means.

ANK'S SHAFT AND HEAD ... T... MINE
ST. IVES CONSOLIDATED ...

GENERAL VIEW OF AIR COMP HOUSE, HOIST HOUSE, FRANKS HEAD-GEAR
BALANCE BOB HOUSE, AND DRY GIEW MINE ST IVES CONSOLIDATED LIMITED. 81

St Ives Consolidated Mines Ltd. Giew section. Frank's Shaft. A further view of the operations. This photograph was taken at the same time as the previous one, *c*.1909. The temporary headgear and capstan shears are in front of the old pumping engine house. To the right are the winding engine and compressor houses.

FRANK'S AIR COMPRESSER GIEW MINE ST. IVES CON. LTD. 62

St Ives Consolidated Mines Ltd. Giew section. Frank's Shaft, *c*.1909. A view inside the compressor house.

St Ives Consolidated Mines Ltd. Giew section. Frank's Shaft, c.1909. The electric winding engine with, on the right, part of the electrically driven air compressor.

St Ives Consolidated Mines Ltd. Giew section. Inside the mill showing buddles and round frames, c.1912.

COLCYNER FLEW AND STACK ROBINSONS HEAD GEAR AND THE MILL GIEW SECTION
ST IVES CONSOLIDATED MINES LTD.

St Ives Consolidated Mines Ltd. Giew section, *c*.1910. The mill which housed twenty head of Californian stamps and the dressing floors. In the foreground is the arsenic calciner flue and stack. The headgear on Robinson's shaft is visible in the background.

TIN YARD AND COLCYNER, GIEW, ST. IVES CONSOLIDATED MINES LTD. CORNWALL

St Ives Consolidated Mines Ltd. Giew section, *c*.1912. The arsenic calciner and tin yard with the long flue connecting the calciner to the stack.

St Ives Consolidated Mines Ltd. Giew section. Robinson's Shaft, *c*.1909. An early photograph taken before the crusher plant was built to the right of the headgear. This crusher served both Frank's Shaft and Robinson's Shaft.

St Ives Consolidated Mines Ltd., Giew section. The Californian stamps and buildings being erected with the mill floors in the foreground, *c*.1909. Robinson's Shaft is visible in the background.

St Ives Consolidated Mines Ltd. Giew section. Skip Road shaft and hoist house, *c.*1909.

St Ives Consolidated Mines Ltd. The Central Power Station, *c.*1911.

St Ives Consolidated Mines Ltd. St Ives Consols section, Sump Shaft headgear. The derelict building to the right is the remains of the pumping engine house in an earlier working, *c.*1910.

St Ives Consolidated Mines Ltd. An internal view of the Central Power Station, *c.*1910.

St Ives Consolidated Mines Ltd. A further view of the Central Power Station, c.1910. There were four diesel engines (four-cylinder vertical type) coupled direct to 135-kilowatt three-phase alternators.

St Ives Consolidated Mines Ltd. A general view of the Giew section, *c*.1912. Top left is the old beam winding engine house which formerly wound from Frank's Shaft. The very tall headgear is on Frank's Shaft with the former pumping engine house being used as an ore bin. To the right and nearer the camera is Robinson's Shaft headgear and, further right, the Californian Mill building. The hip roof building houses the Brunton calciner from which the flue runs to the square brick stack. Skip Road Shaft is centre left. The poles supporting the overhead electricity conductors are prominent.

St Ives Consolidated Mines Ltd. Trenwith section, Victory Shaft, *c*.1912. This was at one time a copper mine that also produced pitchblende (the ore of uranium) in this early twentieth century re-working. The lode was said to have been developing into a tin producer in depth. The advent of the First World War and the consequent call-up of many miners who were Naval Reservists caused the company to concentrate their remaining resources in men and materials at the Giew section. Trenwith and the old St Ives Consols were abandoned.

CONSTRUCTION OF BALL MILL TRENWITH ST IVES CONSOLIDATED LTD.

St Ives Consolidated Mines Ltd. Trenwith section. A ball mill being installed, *c.*1910.

St Ives Consolidated Mines Ltd. St Ives Consols section. East Virgin Shaft headgear and winder house under construction. Note the drums of the electric winder to be installed in the framed-up building, *c.*1909.

St Ives Consolidated Mines Ltd. Trenwith section. Victory Shaft, *c.*1910. The headgear and tramroad in the last re-working.

SUMP HEAD-GEAR ST. IVES CONSOLIDATED LTD. 69

St Ives Consolidated Mines Ltd. St Ives Consols section, *c.*1909. Sump Shaft headgear being erected. Note the remains of the old engine house and boiler house. In the background on the left the headgear on Victory Shaft of Trenwith Mine can be seen. This was also being re-opened at this time.

North Wheal Providence, St Ives. A most interesting photograph from the 1880's showing St Ives Railway station with broad gauge track (7ft$\frac{1}{4}$in). The engine house on the point was erected to serve a shaft which was never sunk! It remained *in situ* for many years. Note the vast amount of shipping in the harbour.

North Wheal Providence, St Ives. A further view of the engine house and harbour this time from the 1870's.

East Providence Mine, Carbis Bay, early 1880's. A view from the valley at Carbis Bay looking seaward. The unusual engine house with a gable end on the bob wall was situated above the St Ives branch of the Great Western Railway.

Providence Mines, Carbis Bay, c.1880. The Count House is the third building from the left-hand edge of the picture and is now a dwelling house. The scene shows the remains of the engine houses and other buildings shortly after this once rich mine had closed.

# *Three*
# Marazion to Hayle

Wheal Grey, Tresowes, c.1923. A china clay pit which was already closed at the time this photograph was taken. The building to the rear of the engine house was possibly used in connection with the clay processing.

Wheal Grey, Tresowes, *c.*1923. A further view of the pumping engine at this clay pit.

Greatwork Mine, Wheal Breage Shaft, *c*.1935. The headgear appears to be complete except for the second sheave wheel. The transformer for the electricity supply can be seen standing behind the winder house. The 'tropical-style' office with a veranda is visible on the left.

Greatwork Mine, Wheal Breage section, Barker's Shaft, *c*.1935. Early operations when the shaft was refurbished in the last re-working. The small single-drum electric winder had been fabricated in sections for use underground at Wheal Buller, near Redruth. It was purchased after Wheal Buller closed and utilized as a surface winder at Greatwork.

Greatwork Mine, Wheal Breage section, Barker's Shaft, c.1935. The headgear and buildings are being erected.

Greatwork Mine, late nineteenth century. A panoramic view looking towards Godolphin Hill showing, from left to right: Leeds Engine Shaft 60-in pumping engine, the large beam winding engine with the carpenters shop, blacksmiths shop, Count House, etc., the burning house stack, the stamps engine house and free standing stack.

Greatwork Mine in the late nineteenth century. The stamps and dressing floors. The beam whim can be seen in the background.

Greatwork Mine. Shafts in the western part of the mine in another late nineteenth-century photograph.

Greatwork Mine, Leeds Engine Shaft, late nineteenth century. The only known print of the engine when at work. A group of miners and surface workers are visible in the foreground.

Greatwork Mine, Leeds Engine Shaft, 1930's. Some of the plant installed in the last re-working. From left to right: steam hoist house, ore bin and headgear. The engine house which formerly contained a 60-in pumping engine has been cut down and provided with a flat roof.

Greatwork Mine, Wheal Reeth Shaft in the western part of the Greatwork sett in a photograph from the 1930's. In the partially-constructed house the gear work of the electrically-driven Cornish pump is visible. This was later dismantled and re-erected to drive the double rod pumping plant at the new South Shaft of the Castle-an-Dinas mine using diesel engines in the Second World War.

Greatwork Mine, Wheal Breage Shaft, 1930's. The house containing the electric winder is nearly completed and the steel headgear has been erected over the shaft. Leeds Shaft pumping engine house is visible in the background.

Greatwork Mine, Leeds Engine Shaft. The plant while being installed in the 1930's re-working.

Greatwork Mine. A 1930's view from the side of the valley showing, from left to right: Leeds Shaft engine house; new steel headgear on Wheal Breage Shaft; the stamps engine house and stack.

Greatwork Mine, Deerpark Shaft, while the wooden headgear was being erected in the 1930's.

Greatwork Mine, Leeds Engine Shaft. A later photograph showing the erection of the new plant nearing completion in the last 1930's re-working.

Greatwork Mine, Deerpark Shaft, c.1937. An electric sinking pump was used to un-water the mine. Steam power was used for hoisting and a steam capstan was employed. These were both housed in the building on the left.

Greatwork Mine, Deerpark Shaft, 1930's. Steam hoist and wooden headgear.

WHEL MIRTH NR. ST. IVES

Wheal Merth, Canonstown, *c*.1905. This re-opening was short-lived. It employed a new horizontal pumping engine built by the Tuckingmill Foundry Co. at Camborne. After closure, the pumping plant was re-erected at Wheal Coates, St Agnes, on Towanrath Shaft (*c*.1911) and was finally moved to Poldice Mine, near St Day, in 1915. The author's father, the late H.K. Bullen, was involved in the manufacture of this engine. He served an engineering apprenticeship with the Tuckingmill Foundry Co.

*Following page:* Wheal Merth, Canonstown, July 1948. A stope near Engine Shaft. From top to bottom the figures visible in the picture are: Alan Thomas; Honor Clemence; Jean Martin.

Lady Gwendolen Mine, Lady Gwendolen Shaft. The first temporary headgear on the shaft during sinking in the early 1920's.

Lady Gwendolen Mine, Lady Gwendolen Shaft. A slightly later photograph (c.1926) showing the permanent headgear and the waste dump.

Lady Gwendolen Mine. The headgear on Lady Gwendolen Shaft, *c.*1927. The considerable dump of waste rock from the shaft sinking and the mill buildings under construction are visible in this picture.

Lady Gwendolen Mine. The mill and the headgear on Lady Gwendolen Shaft, *c.*1927.

Lady Gwendolen Mine. Lady Katharine's Shaft with the balance box on the kingpost of the electrically-driven Cornish pitwork, *c.*1936. The figure is the late J.H. Trounson, a surveyor with the East Pool & Agar Mine.

Lady Gwendolen Mine, the Californian Mill building during the 1930's. Lady Katharine's Shaft, tramway trestle to crusher and dump. Connecting the crusher and the mill is a very short aerial ropeway.

Lady Gwendolen Mine, Lady Katharine's Shaft during the 1930's. The buildings visible in this picture are, from left to right: the electric winder house, headgear, tramway trestle to crusher station and dump.

Lady Gwendolen Mine. Lady Katharine's Shaft is seen here at an early stage in the erection of the plant during the 1930's.

Lady Gwendolen Mine, Lady Katharine's Shaft. Another 1930's view of the erection of the mill, aerial ropeway, crusher station, etc.

The caption here reads Lady Gwendolen Mine, but it would be more correct to say Wheal Reeth at the time this photograph was taken, c.1913. A small single flue marine boiler providing steam for plant in the diminutive mill when working the dumps.

Lady Gwendolen Mine. As in the previous photograph, this should carry the alternative name of Wheal Reeth. The mine was known under both names at different periods of working. This picture shows the small dressing plant in use when treating the dumps, c.1913.

Lady Gwendolen Mine, the Californian Mill and Lady Gwendolen Shaft in the 1930's. Note on the left the aerial ropeway terminal between the mill and Lady Katharine's Shaft which is out of sight on the left.

Tregurtha Downs Mine. An interesting panorama from the late nineteenth century showing the 80-in pumping engine house on Engine Shaft, the headgear on stack shaft, the Count House, Waterstyle Shaft and the mill buildings in the background.

Tregurtha Downs Mine. The horses were the main subject of this photograph, but in fact this provides us with an excellent view of part of this mine in the late nineteenth century. From left to right we can see the Count House, mill, Stack Shaft headgear and Engine Shaft. The latter is dominated by the house of the 80-in pumping engine and associated boiler house and stack.

Tregurtha Downs Mine in the 1940's. An internal view of the house which had contained the 80-in pumping engine. In recent years this magnificent structure has been converted into a dwelling house.

St Erth Valley Alluvial Workings, 1920's. The white plume in the background is from the steam shovel which was used to excavate the alluvium for treatment at the mill. A horse-worked tramway was used to convey the material to the treatment plant as can be seen in the foreground. It is probably lunch time as the horse is tethered and appears to have his nose-bag on!

St Erth Valley Alluvial Workings. A 1920's view of the steam shovel loading waggons on the tramway.

St Erth Valley Alluvial Workings. A view of the treatment plant, again from the 1920's.

St Erth Valley Alluvial Workings. A further view of the treatment plant from the same period.

St Erth Valley Alluvial Workings, 1920's. The steam shovel working under appalling conditions. It is recorded that, on one occasion, the machine had sunk so low that water entered the fire doors and extinguished the fire!

St Erth Valley Alluvial Workings, 1920's. The steam shovel on the edge of the alluvial deposit.

St Erth Valley Alluvial Workings. A bucket dredge being fitted out in the valley. This photograph pre-dates the operations which took place in the 1920's and was probably taken in 1913.

The National Explosives Works at Hayle during the 1920's. Demolishing one of the many stacks at the very large explosives factory on the Towans between Hayle and Gwithian. In this case the brickwork was taken out for a part of the circumference of the stack and replaced by timber supports. The timber was then set alight and when it burnt through the stack collapsed.

*Following pages:*
*Left:* The National Explosives Works at Hayle. The fire has been lit and, in a short period of time, the workers will move away to a point of safety. One of the buildings of the works can be seen in the background.

*Right:* The National Explosives Works at Hayle. The timber has given way and the stack is falling precisely as planned. At the beginning of the twentieth century this large works employed 1,800 workers. During the First World War it was also credited with supplying ninety-eight per cent of the cordite used by the Royal Navy.

122

The National Explosives Works at Hayle in the early twentieth century. A view of part of the very extensive factory built by the National Explosive Co. The works was served by a narrow gauge railway system of remarkable length and complexity. A standard gauge branch of the Great Western Railway was built from Hayle harbour to the works. For part of the route the trackbed of the former Hayle Railway was brought back into use.

Hayle, the Harbour, at one time the chief mining port in Cornwall, *c.*1900. Harvey & Co.'s large foundry and associated works can be seen spread along the quays and to the right of the railway viaduct. The white smoke in the background is coming from the Mellanear Tin Smelting Works.

Harvey & Co.'s Foundry, Hayle. This picture (*c.*1902) depicts the demolition of the works of probably the most prolific engine and other mining machinery builders in Cornwall. It also shows the great faceplate being scrapped.

Hayle Generating Station. When this new electric power station was commissioned it made possible the construction of distribution lines in a greater part of West Cornwall. In order to carry the lines over the river Hayle quite lofty towers had to be erected to give adequate clearance for shipping using the busy port. One of those towers is seen here while it was being lifted at 10.30 a.m. on Saturday 22 July 1911. The Generating Station stack is visible in the background.

Hayle Generating Station. The tower in the centre has been erected. The photograph was taken from the Lelant side of the river with Hayle Generating Station in the background at 10.25 a.m. on Tuesday 8 August 1911. This major work opened up the opportunity for electricity supplies to the mines of Penwith which hitherto had to generate their own power.